PRAYING WITH THE C

Cπ Θεω Ιсχτρос

Praying with the Church Fathers

An Anthology of the
Wisdom of the Church Fathers on Prayer

With an Introduction by the Thrice Blessed
His Holiness Pope Shenouda III

St. Paul Brotherhood Press
Coptic Orthodox Diocese of Los Angeles, Southern California, and Hawaii

PRAYING WITH THE CHURCH FATHERS

Saint Paul Brotherhood Press

—⟋⟍⟍—

Coptic Orthodox Diocese of Los Angeles, Southern California, and Hawaii
Saint Paul Brotherhood
38740 Avenida La Cresta
Murrieta, California 92562
www.SaintPaulBrotherhood.org

First Edition, July 2008
Second Edition, September 2017

ISBN 978-0-9800065-3-7
LCCN 2017954152

The effort of bodily prayer can help those not yet granted real prayer of the heart. I am referring to the stretching out of the hands, the beating on the chest, the sincere raising of the eyes towards heaven, deep sighs and constant prostrations. But this is not always feasible when other people are present, and this is when the demons particularly like to launch an attack and, because we have not yet the strength of mind to stand up against them and because the hidden power of prayer is not yet within us, we succumb. So go somewhere apart, if you can, hide for a while in some secret place. If you can, lift up the eyes of your soul, but if not, the eyes of your body. Stand still with your arms in the shape of the cross so that with this sign you may shame and conquer your Amalek (Exodus 17:11).

Saint John Climacus

His Holiness Pope Tawadros II
118th Pope of Alexandria and
Patriarch of the Great See of Saint Mark

His Eminence Metropolitan Serapion
Metropolitan of Los Angeles,
Southern California, and Hawaii

TABLE OF CONTENTS

PREFACE

With great joy and enthusiasm we present to you, dear reader, *Praying with the Church Fathers*—an anthology of the wisdom of the fathers on prayer.

Prayer and theology should be deeply integrated into the life of every Christian. This echoes the maxim of Evagrius of Pontus: "The one who truly prays is a theologian, and the true theologian is one who prays." Understanding this well, our great ecumenical fathers - such as Saint Athanasius, Saint Cyril, Saint Basil, Saint John Chrysostom, Saint Gregory, Mar Ephrem the Syrian, and many others - delivered a rich tradition of prayers that was passed on from generation to generation so that the pure Orthodox faith could be experienced, practiced and perfected through a life of prayer and worship.

Unfortunately, this rich tradition of prayer has become scarce in the world today. Our glorious Church has uniquely preserved the daily prayers in the Book of Hours and Psalmody in its tradition for all believers. Along with that rich life of prayer, we offer this small companion and guide to assist in the daily practice of continual prayer for all.

The purpose of this work is to provide the faithful with a veritable library of prayers by our great Fathers to continue praying *with* them in the same spirit, zeal and depth. As we commemorate their exemplary lives on earth and contemplate the reward they received - that "which an eye has not seen nor ear heard" – we adopt their spiritual words of prayer and incorporate them into our own lives so that we may emulate them and be worthy of the heavenly reward

We thank all who labored for the preparation, collection, typesetting, editing, publication, and distribution of this work; may the Lord reward them abundantly with the heavenly instead of the earthly.

We hope and pray that this little book motivates the reader to pray, and pray deeply with the example that our Lord Jesus Christ taught us and in the ways the fathers have kept and practiced.

Glory be to the Holy Trinity.

Metropolitan Serapion

I
INTRODUCTION

"Dialogue with the Lord"

Thrice-Blessed His Holiness Pope Shenouda III[1]

"'Come now, let us reason together,' says the Lord" (Isa. 1:18). "Righteous are You, O Lord, when I plead with You; yet let me talk with You about Your judgments. Why does the way of the wicked prosper? Why are those happy who deal so treacherously" (Jer. 12:1). "Lord, how they have increased who trouble me! Many are they who rise up against me. Many are they who say to my soul, 'There is no salvation for him in his God'" (Psa. 3:1, 2). "Why do You stand afar off, O Lord? Why do You disregard me in times of affliction?" (Psa. 9:22). "Shall not the Judge of all the earth do right? Would You also destroy the righteous with the ungodly, so that the righteous should be as the wicked?" (Gen. 18:23-25).

So, Lord, permit me also to enter into dialogue with You. O Lord, You did not create man to perish (St. Athanasius), it would have been better for man to have not been created than to be created to perish. "God desires all men to be saved and to come to the knowledge of the truth" (1 Tim. 2:4). "'Do I ever will the death of a lawless man' says the Lord God, 'since My will is for him to turn from his way and live?'" (Ezek. 18:23). "What profit is there in my blood, when I go down into destruction? Will the dust give praise to You? Or will it declare Your truth?" (Psa. 29:10).

---

[1] The following prayer is based on the sermon delivered by His Holiness Pope Shenouda III on June 24, 1998 at St. Mark's Cathedral, translated by St. Mark Coptic Orthodox Church of Boston, MA; used with gracious permission.

Therefore, if You desire the salvation of everybody, then salvation must come from You. I know very well that You have been crucified for the salvation of the whole world. And You said, "The Son of Man has come to save that which was lost" (Mt. 18:11). But there are many who are not saved, many were lost, and many perish everyday. You Yourself said, "Unless you repent you will all likewise perish" (Lk. 13:3). Why do You permit the devil to exalt himself and widen his kingdom? "It was granted to him to make war with the saints and to overcome them" (Rev. 13:7). And You said concerning the end of the days, "Unless those days were shortened, no flesh would be saved" (Mt. 24:22). It was said that, "Satan will be released from his prison and will go out to deceive the nations" (Rev. 20:7, 8).

O Lord, why are Your children cast down everyday? "Sin has cast down many wounded, and all who were slain by her were strong men" (Prov. 7:26). "Lord, how they have increased who trouble me! Many are they who rise up against me. Many are they who say of me, 'There is no help for him in God'" (Psa. 3:1, 2). Everyday I pray to You, "Make haste, O God, to deliver me! Make haste to seek my soul!" (Psa. 69:1). "In the way in which I was going they have secretly set a snare for me. I look on my right hand and saw, for there is no one who acknowledges me; refuge failed me, and there was no one who cared for my soul" (Psa. 141:4, 5).

O Lord, I am searching for Your will, but I do not know the way to find it. But I say the words of the Psalmist, "Make me know, O Lord, the way in which I should walk... Teach me to do Your will, for You are my God; let Your good Spirit lead me in the land of

uprightness" (Psa. 142:8-10). "I am a sojourner on the
earth; do not hide Your commandments from me" (Psa.
118:19). "Blessed are You, O Lord, teach me Your justice.
Blessed are You, O Lord, make me understand Your rights.
Blessed are You, O Lord, enlighten me in Your
righteousness. Teach me to carry out Your will. Ease our
life and guide us to carry out Your commandments" (The
Coptic Agpeya). "Lead us, throughout the way into to
Your kingdom" (The Divine Liturgy).

Many times have I fallen and strayed from You, but
You asked me, "Return to Me, and I will return to you"
(Mal. 3:7). And I would like to discuss this issue with You.
How can we return to You unless You return to us to bring
us back to You and return us to Yourself? From where do
we start? From ourselves or would You make the start? It
was impossible for the lost sheep to return to You unless
You went searching for him. It was impossible for the lost
coin to return of itself to Your money bag unless You
returned it back to Yourself.

Adam, who escaped from You and hid behind the
trees, was unable to return by himself to You. It was You
Who returned to him and found him and returned him
back. Jonah who escaped from You; it was You Who
returned him back. Elijah who escaped in the wilderness
could not return unless You brought him back. Thomas
doubted Your Resurrection, and it was You Who came to
him and not he who returned to You. The disciples, when
they were afraid and hiding, You returned to them and
brought them back to You. Saul of Tarsus, the persecutor
of the Church, was not the one who returned to You, but it
was You Who returned and brought him back to You.

Still, You say, "Return to Me, and I will return to you" (Mal. 3:7). Lord, return to us to bring us back to You. We alone do not know how to return, as You said, "For without Me you can do nothing" (Jn. 15:5). You also said, "Unless the Lord builds the house, those who build it labor in vain; unless the Lord guards the city, the watchmen stay awake in vain" (Psa. 126:1).

How can we build up our spiritual life without You? How can we guard ourselves against attacks of the devils unless You guard us? The initiative is Yours, not ours. You ask us to repent. Can we repent of ourselves? Or should we say, "Grant me repentance, and I will repent" (Jer. 31:18). I want to repent, but without You I cannot. This is Your divine task because You are the Good Shepherd "Who makes me lie down in green pastures and leads me beside the quiet waters. You restore my soul and guide me in the path of righteousness. Even though I walk through the valley of the shadow of death, I fear no evil for You are with me" (Psa. 22:2-4).

O Lord, You said, "'I Myself will be the Shepherd of My sheep, and I will make them lie down,' says the Lord God. 'I will seek the lost, and I will bring back the strayed, and I will bind up the injured, and I will strengthen the sick'" (Ezek. 34:15, 16). The lost sheep will never return by himself. The driven away cannot return of himself, and the broken cannot bind himself up. Did You not promise, "Lo, I am with you always, even to the end of the age" (Mt. 28:20)? "The gates of Hades shall not prevail against it" (Mt. 16:18). "See, I have inscribed you on the palms of My hands; you are continually before Me" (Isa. 49:16). "Even if a woman forgets her nursing child, yet I will not forget you" (Isa. 49:15).

You promised, "My sheep hear My voice, and I know them, and they follow Me. And I give them eternal life, and they shall never perish; neither shall anyone snatch them out of My hand" (Jn. 10:27, 28). O my Lord, those who snatch are many, and many of Your children are lost. Lord, You said, "Narrow is the gate and difficult is the way which leads to life, and there are few who find it" (Mt. 7:14). O Lord, why are they few who find it, why are they few who are saved, and You said that, "God desires all men to be saved and to come to the knowledge of the truth" (1 Tim. 2:4). Is it not You Who said to Your Father, "Those whom You gave me, and none of them is lost" (Jn. 17:12)?

We plead to You, O Lord, because You are a compassionate God Who does not have any pleasure that the wicked should die, but rather returns and live. We beseech You because You are a Mighty God Who can rescue all. We beg You because You are a Righteous God Who saves the sinners. We implore You because You are gentle and lowly in heart Who allows us to enter into dialogue with You. We entreat You because You are a Wise and Prudent God Who brings out of the strong something sweet. Corruption prevails all over the earth, and this is Your time to work and bring out something sweet. Show us Your strength, show us Your mercy, and grant us Your salvation. "Spare Your people, O Lord, and do not give Your inheritance to reproach, that the nations should rule over them. Why should they say among the nations, 'Where is their God?'" (Joel 2:17). Just as You worked in the past through Your fiery Spirit, work now O Lord, through the gifts of Your Holy Spirit which You promised, "I will pour out of My Spirit on all flesh, I will show wonders in heaven above and signs on the earth beneath" (Acts 2:18, 19).

I know the problem, it is the free will which You granted us. Mankind abused this free will against themselves. Is there any limit of the free will? Would You leave everybody to destroy themselves by their free will? I know that You do not wish to force us in doing good. But, at least, help us and guide us to do Your will.

You say, "Unless you are converted and become as little children, you will by no means enter the kingdom of heaven" (Mt. 18:3). Let it be, treat us as Your little children. A child needs one who carries and bears with him. So carry us and bear with us. A child needs one who guides and feeds him. So guide us and feed us. A child needs one who cleanses. So cleanse us. Consider us like the sick man of Bethesda, who had no man to put him into the pool. You intervened and healed him without a pool. Treat us as weak and crippled sick people. From You comes our strength. My strength and my praise is God, Who has become my salvation.

O Lord, You say, "How often I wanted...but you were not willing!" (Mt. 23:37). If we are not willing, are You going to leave us in our unwillingness? Saint Paul said that the evil I wish not to do, that I practice (cf. Rom. 7:19). Therefore it is no longer I who do it, but sin that dwells in me. Would You let sin abide in us?

But it is You, O God, Who works in us to will and to do for Your good pleasure. If we were not willing, please make us willing. And if we are not doing, help us to do Your will. You are able to give us this will. If we do not wish to live in holiness, give us this desire as a free gift.

Truly, O God, many are those who are fallen and they long to rise, but they cannot. So, raise them and comfort them and look upon Your creation in their weaknesses. You can do everything in everybody. You are all in all and let Your will be done. Amen.

II
THE FOUNDATIONS OF PRAYER FROM A-Z

"The Agpeya Prayers"

Saint Athanasius the Apostolic

I once talked with a certain studious old man, who had bestowed much labor on the Psalter, and discoursed to me about it with great persuasiveness and charm, expressing himself clearly too, and holding a copy of it in his hand while he spoke. So I am going to write down for you the things he said.

Son, all the books of Scripture, both Old Testament and New, are inspired by God and useful for instruction, as the Apostle says; but to those who really study it the Psalter yields especial treasure. Within it are represented and portrayed in all their great variety the movements of the human soul. It is like a picture, in which you see yourself portrayed and seeing, may understand and consequently form yourself upon the pattern given. In the Psalter you learn about yourself. You find depicted in it all the movements of your soul, all its changes, its ups and downs, its failures and recoveries. Moreover, whatever your particular need or trouble, from this same book you can select a form of words to fit it, so that you do not merely hear and then pass on, but learn the way to remedy your ill. Prohibitions of evildoing are plentiful in Scripture, but only the Psalter tells you how to obey these orders and refrain from sin...

But the marvel with the Psalter is that, barring those prophecies about the Savior and some about the Gentiles, the reader takes all its words upon his lips as though they were his own, written for his special benefit, and takes them and recites them, not as though someone else were speaking or another person's feelings being described, but as himself speaking of himself, offering the words to God as his own heart's utterance, just as though he himself had made them up.

It is possible for us, therefore to find in the Psalter not only the reflection of our own soul's state, together with precept and example for all possible conditions, but also a fit form of words with which to please the Lord on each of life's occasions, words both of repentance and of thankfulness, so that we fall not into sin; for it is not for our actions only that we must give account before the Judge, but also for our every idle word.

When you would give thanks to God at your affliction's end, sing Psalm 4, Psalm 75, and Psalm 116. When you see the wicked wanting to ensnare you and you wish your prayer to reach God's ears then wake up early and sing Psalm 5. For victory over the enemy and the saving of created things, take not glory to yourself but, knowing that it is the Son of God who has thus brought things to a happy issue, say to Him Psalm 9; and when you see the boundless pride of man, and evil passing great, so that among men (so it seems) no holy thing remains, take refuge with the Lord and say Psalm 12. And if this state of things be long drawn out, be not fainthearted, as though God had forgotten you, but call upon Him with Psalm 27.

If you want to know how Moses prayed, you have the 90th Psalm. When you have been delivered from these enemies and oppressors, then chant Psalm 18; and when you marvel at the order of creation and God's good providence therein and at the holy precepts of the law, Psalm 19 and Psalm 24 will voice your prayer; while Psalm

20 will give you words to comfort and to pray with others in distress. When you yourself are fed and guided by the Lord and seeing it rejoice, the 23rd Psalm awaits you. Do enemies surround you? Then lift up your heart to God and say Psalm 25, and you will surely see the sinners put to rout. And when you want the right way of approach to God in thankfulness, with spiritual understanding sing Psalm 29... So, then, my son, let whoever reads this book of Psalms take the things in it quite simply as God-inspired. In every case the words you want are written down for you, and you can say them as your own. [2]

"BOLDNESS IN PRAYER"

MAR ISAAC THE SYRIAN

Sit in the presence of the Lord every moment of your life, as you think of Him and recollect Him in your heart. Otherwise, when you only see Him after a period of time, you will lack freedom of converse with Him, out of shame; for great freedom of converse is born out of constant association with Him. Constant association with fellow-beings involves the body, whereas when it is with God, it involves the soul's meditation and the offering of prayers. As a result of its great intensity, this meditation is sometimes mingled with wonder: 'Let the heart of those who seek the Lord rejoice' (Psalm 104:3). Seek the Lord, O sinners, and be strengthened in your thoughts with hope. Seek His face through repentance at all times - and you shall be sanctified by the holiness of His face. You shall be purged clean of your wickedness. Run to the Lord, all you who are wicked; He forgives wickedness and removes sins.

---

[2] *Excerpts from the Letter to Marcellinus.*

"THE BLESSING OF PRAYER"

SAINT GREGORY OF NYSSA

The effect of prayer is union with God, and if someone is with God, he is separated from the enemy. Through prayer we guard our chastity, control our temper, and rid ourselves of vanity. It makes us forget injuries, overcome envy, defeat injustice, and makes amends for sin. Through prayer we obtain physical well-being, a happy home, and a strong, well-ordered society. It will refresh you when you are weary and comfort you when you are sorrowful. Prayer is the delight of the joyful as well as the solace of the afflicted.[3]

SAINT JOHN CHRYSOSTOM

Prayer is a great blessing...both when we receive what we ask and when we do not receive it. For when He gives and when He does not give, He does it for your good. Thus when you receive what you ask, it is quite clear that you have received it; but when you do not receive it, you also receive, because you thus do not receive what is undoubtedly harmful for you; and not to receive what is harmful means to be granted what is useful. So whether you receive what you ask or not, give thanks to God in the belief that God would have always given us what we ask were it not often better for us not to receive it. Prayer is a great weapon, a rich treasure, a wealth that is never exhausted, an undisturbed refuge, a cause of tranquility, the root of a multitude of blessings and their source. [4]

---

[3] *Homilies On the Lord's Prayer,* Sermon 1.
[4] *Concerning the Statutes,* Homily 1.31.

"CAPTIVATED IN PRAYER"

SAINT MACARIUS THE GREAT

A maiden espoused to a wealthy man may receive any number of gifts before the consummation: ornaments, clothing, or precious vessels. But she is not satisfied until the time of the marriage comes and she arrives at full communion. So the soul, betrothed to the heavenly Bridegroom, receives as pledge from the Spirit gifts of healing, of knowledge, or of revelation. But it is not satisfied with these until it reaches the perfect communion, that is, of love unchangeable and unfailing. It frees from passion and agitation those who have desired it. So also, an infant might be decked out with pearls and costly clothing. When he is hungry, he thinks nothing of the things he wears, and cares only for the breast of his nurse—how it may receive milk. So also consider it to be with the spiritual gifts of God to Whom be glory forever. Amen. [5]

"DOVE'S WINGS IN PRAYER"

SAINT GREGORY OF NYSSA[6]

When you pray, say: "Our Father, Who art in Heaven." In one of the psalms the great David asks, "Who will give me wings like a dove?" (Psalm 54:7). I too, would boldly use the same words. Who is there to give those wings by which my mind might take its flight to the heights envisioned in the noble words of this petition? Leaving behind all that is of earth, I would advance and move through the middle air. I would attain to the beauty

---

[5] *Spiritual Homilies* 45.7.
[6] *Homilies on the Lords Prayer*, Sermon 1.

of the ethereal space, reach the stars, and contemplate their order and arrangement. However, I would not stop even there. Progressing beyond them, I would abandon as alien everything subject to movement and change. Then I would, at last, perceive that Nature which is immutable, the unchanging Power existing in its own right, as it guides and sustains all things in being - for all are dependent on the ineffable will of Divine Wisdom. Thus, must my mind, detached from all that is subject to motion, flux and change, come to rest quietly in spiritual repose without movement. Then will I be made like Him who is perfectly unchangeable. Then I will be able to address Him by that intimate name and say, "Father."

What spirit must there be in a person who would pronounce this word! What trust! What a pure conscience! Let us suppose that a man might seek to know God as much as possible, by considering the names that have been invented for the Deity and thus arrive at an understanding of God's ineffable glory. That man would learn that whatever the Divine Nature is in itself, it is absolute goodness, holiness, joy, power, glory, and purity. It is eternity, absolutely and always the same. Considering these things and all things besides that thought could learn through the acred Scriptures or through meditation, could anyone dare to utter this word and call God Father? If a man has any sense, he would surely not dare to call God by this name, Father, since he does not find in himself the things he sees in God.

Therefore, if the Lord in His prayer teaches us to call God Father, it would seem that what He is doing is giving us as our law the most sublime law. Truth does not teach us to deceive by saying we are something we are not or by using a name to which we have no claim. Therefore, it is dangerous for us to dare to offer this prayer and to call God our Father before our lives have been purified.

At one time, we humans as intelligent beings were healthy; for the movements of our soul, which correspond to the elements of the universe, were balanced evenly within us in every manner in the harmony of virtue. Then, the element of concupiscence became dominant, defeating its opposite, continence, as a strong enemy overpowers a conquered warrior. No longer were the inordinate desires for things forbidden held in check. In this way, the fatal disease of sin was introduced into our human nature. For this reason, the true Physician of the diseases of our soul shared our life so as to heal those who were ill. He gradually lessens the root of the disease through the meaning of this prayer. Thus we are restored by Him to spiritual health.

"Elevated Hands"

The Scholar Tertullian

But we more commend our prayers to God when we pray with modesty and humility, with not even our hands too loftily elevated, but elevated temperately and becomingly; and not even our countenance over-boldly uplifted. For that publican who prayed with humility and dejection not merely in his supplication, but in his countenance too, went his way "more justified" than the shameless Pharisee. The sounds of our voice, likewise, should be subdued; or else, if we are to be heard for our noise, how large windpipes should we need! But God is the hearer not of the voice, but of the heart, just as He is its inspector. Do the ears of God wait for sound? How then could Jonah's prayer find way out unto heaven from the depth of the whale's belly, through the entrails of so huge a beast; from the very abyss, through so huge a mass of sea? What superior advantage will they who pray also loudly gain, except that they annoy their neighbors? No, by making their petitions audible, what less error do they commit than if they were to pray in public? [7]

"FAITHFUL PRAYER"

SAINT JOHN CHRYSOSTOM

Our talk is about prayer, in which alone the soul offers to God from its depths. It is a kind of spiritual wealth. All acts of justice which a person does, that person does according to his capability and brings them forth from the store of his capacity. His prayer alone speaks according to his faith and brings forth from the store of his faith. Do you want to know how precious prayer is? No act of outward justice is compared with incense, only prayer is. As is shown in the Revelation of John, the great angel proceeds before the visage of the altar, holding in his hand a censer of the fragrances of incense, and it is said to him, "These are the prayers of the saints" (Revelation 5:8). Just as well- blended incense delights the worshipful person, so the prayer of the just person is sweet before God. Do you wish to know its dignity? As soon as it issues from the mouth, the angels take it up in their hands and bring it before God, just as the archangel said to Tobias, "I am he

---

[7] "Of Elevated Hands," *Treatise on Prayer*, ANF v. 3, Ch. 17.

who has brought your prayer before the Holy One" (Tobit 12:15).[8]

"FIXED TIMES FOR PRAYER"

SAINT JEROME

Though the Apostle commands us to pray unceasingly (1 Thessalonians 5:17), and although saints' sleep itself is also considered prayer, yet we should put certain fixed hours for prayers, so that if we are absorbed in work, this fixed time of prayer would remind us of our duty. Everyone knows that prayer is to be held at the third, sixth, ninth, and eleventh hour, and at dawn.[9]

"FEAR AND PRAYER"

MAR ISAAC THE SYRIAN

To keep the thought of God always in your mind you must cling totally to this formula for piety: 'Come to help me, O God; Lord, hurry to my rescue!' (Psalm 69:2). It carries within it all the feelings of which human nature is capable. It carries within it a cry of help to God in the face of every danger. It expresses the humility of a pious confession. It conveys the watchfulness born of unending worry and fear. It can be adapted to every condition, and can be usefully deployed against every temptation. Someone forever calling out to his Protector is indeed very sure of having Him close by.[10]

---

[8] *Incomplete work on Matthew*, Homily 13.5.

[9] *Epistle* 22:37, cf. *Epistles* 107:9, 108:20, 130:15.

[10] *On Prayer*, Conference 10.

"Golden Prayer"

Saint John Chrysostom

There is nothing more worthwhile than to pray to God and to converse with Him, for prayer unites us with God as His companions. As our bodily eyes are illuminated by seeing the light, so in contemplating God our soul is illuminated by Him. Of course, the prayer I have in mind is no matter of routine; it is deliberate and earnest. It is not tied down to a fixed timetable; rather it is a state which endures by night and day.

Our soul should be directed in God, not merely when we suddenly think of prayer, but even when we are concerned with something else. If we are looking after the poor, if we are busy in some other way, or if we are doing any type of good work, we should season our actions with the desire and the remembrance of God. Through this salt of the love of God we can all become a sweet dish for the Lord. If we are generous in giving time to prayer, we will experience its benefits throughout our life.

Prayer is the light of the soul, giving us true knowledge of God. It is a link mediating between God and man. By prayer the soul is borne up to heaven and in a marvelous way embraces the Lord. This meeting is like that of an infant crying on its mother, and seeking the best of milk. The soul longs for its own needs and what it receives is better than anything to be seen in the world.

Prayer is a precious way of communicating with God; it gladdens the soul and gives repose to its affections. You should not think of prayer as being a matter of words. It is a desire for God, an indescribable devotion, not of human origin, but the gift of God's grace. As Saint Paul says, "We do not know what we should pray for as we ought, but the Spirit Himself makes intercession for us with groanings which cannot be uttered" (Romans 8:26).

Anyone who receives from the Lord the gift of this type of prayer possesses a richness that is not to be taken from him, a heavenly food filling up the soul. Once he has tasted this food, he is set alight by an eternal desire for the Lord, the fiercest of fires lighting up his soul.

To set about this prayer, paint the house of your soul with modesty and lowliness and make it splendid with the light of justice. Adorn it with the beaten gold of good works and, for walls and stones, embellish it assiduously with faith and generosity. Above all, place prayer on top of this house as its roof so that the complete building may be ready for the Lord. Thus He will be received in a splendid royal house and by grace His image will already be settled in your soul. [11]

"HARMONY IN PRAYER"

THE STRONG ABBA MOSES

Abba Moses once said to Abba Poemen, "If a man's deeds are not in harmony with his prayer, he labors in vain." That brother said, "What is this harmony between practice and prayer?" The old man said, "We should no longer do those things against which we pray. For when a man gives up his own will, then God is reconciled with him and accepts his prayers." The brother asked, "In all the affliction which the monk gives himself, what helps him?"

---

[11] *On Prayer*, Homily 6.

The old man said, "It is written, 'God is our refuge and our strength, a help in afflictions that severely befall us'" (Psalm 45:1).[12]

"HUMBLE PRAYER"

CHROMATIUS

Nonbelievers think that they can more easily obtain from the Lord what they require by using many words, but the Lord does not expect this from us. Rather, He wants us to send up our prayers not with wordy speech but with faith that comes from the heart. By doing so, we command the merits of justice to Him. He surely knows better all the things of which we have need, and before we speak He is aware of everything that we are going to request...

We have an example of just how great a distance there is between the wordy and the humble and simple prayer in the story of the Pharisee and the publican. The prayer of the Pharisee vaunting himself in his abundance of words was rejected. The humble and contrite publican, on the other hand, asking forgiveness for his sins, came away more justified than the self- boasting Pharisee. In this we find fulfilled what was written, "The prayer of the humble pierces the clouds" (Sirach 35:17), reaching God who is ready to hear the request of the one who prays.[13]

---

[12] *Apothegmata Patrum*, Abba Moses [4.14], saying 4.
[13] *Tractate on Matthew* 27.2.1-3.

"THE INNER CHAMBER"

SAINT AUGUSTINE

Enter into your inner chamber. Do not let the door stand open to the boisterous, through whom the things that are outside profanely rush in and assail the inner self...Outside the inner chamber are all things in time and space, which knock on the door. Through our bodily senses they clamor to interrupt our prayer, so that prayer is invaded with a crowd of vain phantoms. This is why you must shut the door. The senses of the body are resisted so that the spirit of prayer may be directed to the Father. This occurs in the inmost heart, where prayer is offered to the Father in secret. There, "your Father Who sees in secret will reward you" (Matthew 6:6, 18).

This is a fitting conclusion to good counsel, not merely calling us to pray but also showing us how; not merely calling us to give alms but also showing the right spirit for doing so. The instruction is to cleanse the heart. Nothing cleanses the heart but the undivided and single-minded, striving after eternal life from the pure love of wisdom alone.[14]

"THE JESUS (OR ARROW) PRAYER"

SAINT MACARIUS THE GREAT

There is no need to waste time with words; it is enough to hold out your hands and say, "Lord, according to Your desire and to Your wisdom, have mercy." If you are hard-pressed in the struggle, say, "Lord, save me!" or say,

---

[14] *Sermon on the Mount* 2.3.11.

"Lord." For He knows what is best for you, and will have mercy upon you.[15]

EVAGRIUS OF PONTUS

At the time of these temptations, make use of short and intense prayer.

"KINGDOM PRAYER"

MAR ISAAC THE SYRIAN

Do not seek from God those things which He is anxious to give us, even when we do not beg for them and which He does not withhold even from those who are wholly alien to any knowledge of Him. Do not use vain repetitions like the pagans do and give no thought saying what shall we eat and what shall we drink or with what shall we be clothed; your Father knows that you also have need of all these things. If your Father takes care of the birds, how much more will He take care of you? But ask from God the Kingdom and its righteousness and then He will add these things also.

Someone may ask, "Why do these great and ineffable gifts only occur at this time of prayer?" Our reply is, "It is because at this time, more than at any other, a person is

---

[15] *Apothegmata Patrum*, Abba Macarius [3], saying 19. According to the ancient tradition in the deserts Egypt, the monks of old would make such petitions that became known as "Arrow prayers" including those such as "Lord, make haste to help me," "Lord, make speed to save me," or the famous prayer:
"O my Lord Jesus Christ have
mercy on me. O my Lord Jesus
Christ help me. O my Lord Jesus
Christ, I glorify You."

recollected and in a state of preparedness to gaze towards God, yearning and hoping for mercy from Him." In brief, it is the time when a person is standing at the King's door, making his request, and it is appropriate that the request of someone who supplicates with real desire should be accorded to him then. For when is a person so attentive and in such a state of readiness and preparedness, as he is at the time when he prays?

"LIGHTHOUSE OF PRAYER"

SAINT AMBROSE OF MILAN

In prayer, let your door stand open to receive Him; unlock your soul to Him; offer Him a welcome in your mind, and then you will see the riches of simplicity, the treasures of peace, joy, and grace. Throw wide the gate of your heart, stand before the Sun in everlasting light that shines on every man. This true Light shines on all, but if anyone closes his window, he will deprive himself of eternal Light. If you shut the door of your mind, you shut out Christ. Although He can enter, He does not want to force His way in rudely, or compel us to admit Him against our own will.

"LITTLE BY LITTLE"

SAYINGS OF THE DESERT FATHERS

Once an Abba told a discouraged brother the following story: "A man had a plot of land and through his carelessness brambles sprang up and it became a wilderness of thistles and thorns. Then he decided to cultivate it. So he said to his son, 'Go and clear that ground.' So the son went to clear it, and saw that the thistles and thorns had multiplied...He said, 'How much time shall I need to clear and weed all this?' And he lay on the ground and went to sleep. He did this day after day. Later, his father came to see what he had done and found him doing nothing. When his father asked him about it, the son replied that the job had looked so hard that he could never make himself begin. His father replied, 'Son, if you had cleared each day the area on which you lay down your work you would have advanced slowly and you would not have lost heart.' So the lad did what his father said, and in a short time the plot was cultivated." So the Abba told the discouraged brother, "Do a little work and do not faint, and God will give you grace."

"THE MIND'S ASCENT IN PRAYER"

EVAGRIUS OF PONTUS

Prayer is an ascent of the mind to God. If you love God, you converse with Him continually as you would with your father, banishing every passion from your mind.

Prayer is the daughter of gentleness.

Prayer is the fruit of joy and gratitude.

Prayer is a continual communication of the spirit with God.

Prayer is the joy that gives rise to thanksgiving.

Prayer makes gentleness blossom in the heart.

Prayer saves from despondency and discouragement.[16]

---

[16] Evagrius (A.D. 346-399) occupied a central place in the history of Christian spirituality. He lived as a monk for two years in Nitria, then fourteen years in the Kellia (or "Cells").

SAINT ANTONY THE GREAT

The mind is not perfectly at prayer until the one praying does not think of himself or know that he is praying.

"NO EXCUSE FOR CONTINUAL PRAYER"

SAINT JOHN CHRYSOSTOM

No one should give the answer that it is impossible for a man occupied with worldly cares to pray always. You can set up an altar to God in your mind by means of prayer. And so it is fitting to pray at your work, on a journey, standing at a counter, or sitting at your handicraft.

"OBEDIENT PRAYER"

SAINT DIDYMUS THE BLIND ("THE SEER")

Now once when [Saint Didymus] was urging me to make a prayer in his cell and I was unwilling to do so, he spoke to me and related to me concerning Abba Anthony who, he said, "Came three times and visited me in this cell. And when I begged and entreated him to pray, immediately he knelt down on his knees, and prayed, and did not waited for me to speak one word about it. But at the first word he corrected me by his obedience. He did not let me finish my speech, but by his work he made manifest obedience." And Didymus said to me, "You also, if you wish to walk in his footsteps and imitate him in his life, deeds, and hospitality, and if you desire to walk in the life of excellence and in the love of God, remove yourself from contention."[17]

"OPENING THE DOOR OF PRAYER"

SAINT JOHN CHRYSOSTOM

These things are better understood in a spiritual sense, as spoken about the soul. The "Room" is the heart, or the inner, that is, spiritual intellect. It has been written, "That which you say in your hearts, also grieve for in private"

The doorway is the exterior, bodily sense through which all things, good and bad, enter upon the soul. So also in the Canticle, Wisdom speaks in the person of the church: "Behold, my beloved knocks at the door, 'Open to me, my sister, my spouse'" (Song 5:2).

Christ also knocks at the door of the Christian, entering the heart either through the divine Scriptures or good thoughts. The one who receives them opens oneself to Christ. The one who sends them away shuts the door. For this reason Jesus orders that the soul enter the inward understanding when it prays, so that it thinks of nothing except for what it prays and to whom it prays. Thus it closes the doorway of its bodily sense, so that it may shut outside all external thoughts and cares.[18]

---

[17] A story told by Saint Didymus the Blind to Saint Palladius, recounted in Chapter 4 of his *Paradise of the Fathers*.

[18] *Incomplete Work on Matthew*, Homily 13.13.

"THE PALACE OF PRAYER"

SAINT JOHN CHRYSOSTOM

When you pray, it is as if you were entering into a palace—not a palace on earth, but far more awesome, a palace in heaven. When you enter there, you do so with complete attentiveness and fitting respect. For in the houses of kings all turmoil is set aside, and silence reigns. Yet here you are being joined by choirs of angels. You are in communion with archangels and singing with the seraphim, who sing with great awe their spiritual hymns and sacred songs to God, the Lord of all. So when you are praying, mingle with these voices, patterning yourself according to their mystical order. It is not to human beings that you are praying, but to God, Who is present everywhere, Who hears even before you speak and Who knows already the secrets of the heart. If you pray to this One, you shall receive a great reward. "For your Father who sees in secret shall reward you openly" (Matthew 6:4). He did not merely say He would give it to you, but reward you, as if He Himself had made a pledge to you and so honored you with a great honor. Because God Himself is hidden, your prayer should be hidden...

While pretending to pray to God, the hypocrites are looking around for human praise. The elaborate garb they wear is laughable, and hardly that of a sincere supplicant. One who is earnestly offering a supplication looks exclusively to the One Who has the power to grant the request and lets all other claims recede. But if you leave behind the One you are petitioning and immediately go wandering about looking everywhere for others' approval, you will depart with empty hands.[19]

"PERSISTENCE IN PRAYER"

SAINT ANTONY THE GREAT

I never get tired of asking the Lord on your behalf, that you may know the grace that has been given you. For God, in His mercy, reminds every one of the means of the grace given to him. So never lose heart or be lazy, my children, in crying to the Lord night and day, that you may force the Father's benevolence to grant you aid from above.

"PRAYING THE PSALMS"

SAINT ATHANASIUS THE GREAT

Each psalm is both spoken and composed by the Spirit so that in these same words... the stirring of our souls might be grasped and all of them be said as concerning us, and (the Psalms) issue from us as our own words...just as He provided the model of the earthly and the heavenly man in His own person, so also from the Psalms he who wants to do so can learn the emotions and dispositions of the soul, finding in them also the therapy and correction suited for each emotion.[20]

---

[19] *On Matthew*, Homily 19.3.
[20] *Letter to Marcellinus*.

"PRAYING FOR PURITY"

AMMA SARAH

If I prayed God that all men should approve of my conduct, I should find myself a penitent at the door of each one, but I shall rather pray that my heart may be pure towards all.[21]

"QUALITY PRAYER"

AN ELDER

You must pray not only with words, but with the mind, and not only with the mind, but with the heart so that the mind understands and sees clearly what is said in words, and the heart feels what the mind is thinking. All these combined together constitute real prayer, and if any of them are absent, your prayer is either not perfect or is not prayer at all.

"PRAYERS FOR REPENTANCE"

SAINT MACARIUS OF ALEXANDRIA[22]

O eternal God, King of all creation, Who have granted me to attain to this hour, forgive me the sins which I have committed this day in thought, word, and deed. Cleanse, O Lord, my humble soul from every stain of flesh and spirit. Grant me, O Lord, to pass through the sleep of this night in peace, that when I rise from my bed I may please Your Holy Name all the days of my life, and conquer the enemies, both those corporeal and incorporeal that contend

---

[21] *Apothegmata Patrum*, Amma Sarah [6], saying 5.
[22] Evening Prayers in Byzantine Tradition attributed to St. Macarius.

against me. Deliver me, O Lord, from the vain thoughts that stain me, and from evil desires. For Your is the kingdom, and the power, and the glory of the Father, and of the Son, and of the Holy Spirit, now and ever, and unto age of all ages. Amen.

SAINT EPHRAIM THE SYRIAN[23]

O Lord and Master of my life, grant not unto me a spirit of idleness, of discouragement, of lust for power, and of vain speaking.But bestow upon me, Your servant, the spirit of chastity, of meekness, of patience, and of love. Yes, O Lord and King, grant that I may perceive my own transgressions, and judge not my brother, for blessed are You unto age of all ages. Amen.

"RULES OF PRAYER"

SAINT ANTONY THE GREAT

And if the mind conquers in this contest, then it prays in the Spirit and begins to expel from the body the passions of the soul which come to it from its own will... And the Spirit teaches the mind how to heal all the wounds of the soul and to rid itself of every one, those which are mingled in the members of the body. And for the eyes it sets a rule, that they may see rightly and purely. After that, it sets a rule also for the ears, how they may hear in peace, and no more thirst or desire to hear ill speaking. but to hear about the mercy shown to the whole creation... Then again, the Spirit teaches the tongue its own purity...and heals the motions of the hands...and instructs the mind in their

---

[23] This prayer is said in Eastern Orthodox services of the Great Fast with three prostrations.

purification, that it may labor with them in almsgiving and in prayer; and the word is fulfilled concerning them which says, "Let the lifting up of my hands be an evening sacrifice" (Psalm 140:2)... And the belly to eat in moderation, sufficient for the strength of the body, and in this way the saying of Paul is fulfilled, "Whether you eat or drink, or whatever you do, do all to the glory of God" (1 Corinthians 10:31). And it gives the feet also their purification. that they should walk according to its will, going and ministering in good works. And I think that when the whole body is purified and has received the fullness of the Spirit, it has received some portion of that spiritual body which it is to assume in the resurrection of the just.

"SAINTLY PRAYER"

SAINT BASIL THE GREAT

God sees into the hearts of those who pray. What need then, someone will say, that we should ask God for what we need? Does He not know already what we need?

Why then should we pray? God certainly knows the things we need, and generously provides all we need for the refreshment of our bodies. Since He is good, He sends down His rain upon the just and unjust, and also causes His sun to shine upon the evil and the good (Matthew 5: 45), even before we ask Him. But you will not receive faith, the power of virtue, and the kingdom of heaven unless you ask for them in laboring and steadfastness.

We must first long for these things. Then when you desire them, you must strive with all your heart to obtain them, seeking them with a sincere heart, with patience, and with faith, not being condemned by your conscience, as praying without attention or without reverence, and so in time, when God wills, you will obtain your request. For He knows better than you when these things are appropriate for you. And maybe He is delaying in giving them to you, designing to keep your attention fixed upon Him; and also that you may know that this is a gift of God, and may safeguard with fear what is given to you. For what we come by with much labor we are zealous to defend; as losing it we lose also our labor; and treating lightly the gift of God we become unworthy of life eternal. For what did it profit Solomon so quickly to receive the gift of wisdom and then lose it?

So do not lose heart if you do not speedily obtain your request. For if it were known to our Good Master that were you at once to receive this favor that you would not lose it, He would have been prepared to give it to you unasked. But being concerned for you, He does not do this. For if he who received a single talent, and hid it safely, was condemned because he did not put it to profit, how much more would he have been condemned had he lost it? Keeping this in mind, let us continue to give thanks to the Lord whether we receive speedily or slowly that which we pray for. For all things whatsoever the Lord may do He orders all to the end of our salvation; only let us not through faintheartedness cease from our prayers. It was because of this the Lord spoke the parable of the widow who persuaded the judge through her steadfastness (Luke 18:2-5), that we also through our steadfastness in prayer may obtain what we ask for.

By this we also show our faith and our love of God, since though we do not quickly receive what we ask for, yet we remain steadfast in praising Him and giving thanks. Then let us give Him thanks at all times, so that we may be found worthy of receiving His everlasting gifts; since to Him all praise and glory is due forever and ever. Amen.[24]

"TEARS IN PRAYER"

MAR EPHREM THE SYRIAN

Do you wish to lead a proper life? Exercise humility, for without it, it is impossible to lead a proper life. Do all your work in the name of our Savior Jesus Christ, and thus shall your fruits be carried up to heaven.

A man begins to go astray when he withdraws from humility. He who has abandoned God does the evil spirit oppress, as he did Saul. The enemy's snares are smeared with honey. He who is attracted by the sweetness of honey becomes caught in the snares and filled with all manner of woe. Love humility and you will never fall into the devil's snare, for soaring on humility's swift wings, you will always remain above the enemy's snares. Arrogance is like a very tall but rotten tree. All of its branches are brittle and if someone climbs upon it, he immediately falls from the height he has attained. Blessed is he who is enriched with good hopes and illuminated with good thoughts: his glory is great and everlasting.

Let us strive for sober attention that we might recognize our sins and be constantly humbled; that we might not nurture, like the serpent, a high opinion of ourselves or wickedness. Let us love sobriety that we might

---

[24] "That Prayer is to be Placed Before All Things," *Monastic Constitutions*, Ch. 1, PG 31.

have a pure heart and that we might preserve the temple entrusted to us undefiled by sinful corruption.

Wondrous is prayer accompanied by sighs and tears, especially if the tears are shed in secret. He who prays in his mind with faith beholds the Lord before himself. For in Him do we live, move, and exist.

If your heart has been hardened, weep before the Lord that He might shine upon you the illumination of knowledge and grant that with an ardent heart you might be carried up to Him.[25]

"THE TEMPLE OF PRAYER"

SAINT IGNATIUS OF ANTIOCH

It is right to glorify Jesus Christ in every way; He has glorified You. I am not giving you an order, as if I were important. For, even if I am in chains for the sake of the Name, I have not yet grown to full stature in Jesus Christ. Only now am I beginning to be His pupil and I speak to you as fellow disciples. I need to be anointed by your faith, your exhortations, your patience, and your forbearance. Each one of you, together, should form a chorus so that in harmonious consonance, taking in unity the note intoned by God, you may, as a single voice, sing a hymn to the Father, through Jesus Christ. He will listen to you and recognize you, through the good works you do, as members of His Son. This is why it is important for you to be inseparable in your unity, so that you may always share in God, Himself.

---

[25] *The Spiritual Psalter.*

You are stones for the Father's temple, hoisted on high by the crane of Jesus Christ, I mean, His Cross, with the Holy Spirit acting as a cable for You. Your faith draws You up; love is the pathway by which You ascend toward God. Thus, all of You are also traveling companions, bearing God, bearing the temple, bearing Christ, bearing sacred vessels. In all things, You adorned with the precepts of Jesus Christ.

Pray without ceasing for others. There is hope that they will repent and come to God. At least, let them become Your disciples because of the works You do. When they are angry, be gentle and mild. When they boast and brag, be humble. When they blaspheme, pray. When they go astray, remain steadfast in faith. When they are brutal, be a peacemaker. Do not seek to become like them. Let us be brothers and sisters to them, showing goodness to them, as we strive to be imitators of the Lord.

Who among us has been the object of most injustice? Who has been the most deprived? Who, most rejected? Let not one of the devil's weeds grow up in Your midst. In all purity and temperance may You abide, body and spirit, in Jesus Christ. Only if we were found to be in Christ will we enter into true life. Have no treasure apart from Him. It is in Him that I wear these chains as spiritual pearls. Would that I might rise, still wearing them, because of Your prayer. In that prayer I hope always to share, as an heir of the Christians in Ephesus, who have always remained united to the Apostles, through the power of Jesus Christ.

Remember me, as Jesus Christ is mindful of You. Pray for the Church in Syria. Keep well in God the Father and in Jesus Christ, Who is the hope we share in common.[26]

"UNITED PRAYER"

SAINT CYPRIAN OF CARTHAGE

Above all else, He Who is the Teacher of peace and the Master of unity did not wish us to pray individually and privately as one would pray for oneself alone. We do not say, "My Father, Who art in heaven." Neither does each one ask that his debt alone be forgiven, nor that she not be led into temptation. No one asks to be delivered from evil for oneself only. Our prayer is public and offered from evil in common. When we pray, it is not for one person, but for the entire people; because, we the whole people are one. God, Who is the Teacher of prayer and peace, taught us peace. He wished each one pray for all, just as He, Himself has borne all together in one.

The three youth in the fiery furnace observed this law. They were united as one in their prayer; they were in harmony with one another in the spirit. The divine Scriptures affirm in faith how they prayed, giving us an example to imitate in our prayers, so that we might become like them. "Then those three, as if with one mouth, sang a hymn, glorified and blessed God" (Daniel 3:51, LXX). They spoke as if with one mouth, although Christ had not yet taught them how to pray. The words they offered in prayer were fruitful and efficacious, because prayer that is full of peace, simple, and spiritual appeals to the Lord.

---

[26] *Epistle to the Ephesians*, §§9, 10.

The apostles and disciples also prayed in this manner, after the Lord's Ascension: "These all continued in one accord in prayer and supplication with the woman and Mary, the mother of Jesus, and with His brethren" (Acts 1:14). With a united mind, they persevered in prayer. By their steadfastness and their unity in prayer, they proclaimed that God, Who makes those who are of one mind to dwell together in one house, admits to the eternal, divine home, only those who are found to be of one mind in prayer.[27]

"VIGIL IN PRAYER"

PARADISE OF THE FATHERS

They used to say about Abba Arsenius that no man was able to attain the manner of life in his residence. They also said that on Saturday evening, he would stretch out his hands toward heaven with the sun behind him, and pray in this position until the sun rose in his face on the dawn of Sunday. Then, he would satisfy his eyes with a little rest...[28]

One day Abba Arsenius called Abba Alexander and Abba Zolla and said to them, "Because the devils are fighting against me and I know that they may carry me off during my sleep, toil here with me this night and keep vigil. Watch me and see if I sleep during my vigil." So they sat down, one on his right hand and the other on his left, from the evening until the morning. And they said, "We slept and arose, but we did not see him sleep at all. But when it began to be light we heard him breathe three times from

---

[27] *Treatise on the Lord's Prayer*, 8-9.

[28] *Paradise of the Fathers*, v. 2, sayings 105 and 113.

his nostrils. We do not know if he did this on purpose so that we might think he slept, or whether sleep had really fallen upon him." Then he stood up and said to us, "Did I sleep?" So we answered and said to him, "We do not know, O father, for we ourselves slept."

"WANDERING THOUGHTS IN PRAYER"

DESERT FATHERS

A brother asked an elder and said, "My thoughts wander and I am troubled." He answered, "Continue sitting in your cell and your thoughts will return from their wanderings. If a donkey is tied, her children skips and jumps all around her but always comes back to the mother. So it will be with the one who for God's sake sits patiently in his cell. Though thoughts wander for a time, they will come again."

THRICE-BLESSED HIS HOLINESS POPE SHENOUDA III[29]

The mind has many functions: thoughts, understanding, memory, and deduction. Saint Isaac the Syrian says wondering thoughts in prayer are not a "matter for beginners." The pure prayer that is completely without any flight of thought needs spiritual maturity. Beginners, when they start to follow the pathway of perfection are usually occupied with many duties and contacts thus there

---

[29] The following is based on a question and answer session by the Thrice-Blessed His Holiness Pope Shenouda III in the 1980s at Saint Pishoy's Monastery, Wadi Natroun, Egypt, translated by Saint Paul Brotherhood.

is so much to occupy the mind and distract it. Saint Isaac continues saying, "the senses are the doors and windows of the thoughts. What one sees, hears, smells, touches, or tastes will make them think about it." In order to control our thoughts we need to start by controlling our senses. Therefore, one should not occupy their scenes more than what is necessary.

In the wilderness, the distraction by the senses are less, so there should be little that can occupy the person's mind. This is not the case for the person who occupies their senses with many distractions.

Practical means of thought control needs a solitary life [may be referred to as quite time for those living within the world], though not everyone is able to master that perfectly. It was said by Saint Isaac the Syrian that there is "...there are some who are shut-in their cells,[30] yet are occupied by selling and buying with their own thoughts." The thoughts of a distracted person accompany them during the day such as certain tasks they did not complete or there may be some discussion with others that were not concluded. Thus one's dealings with others may be a source of arousal for the senses. If one is happy or unhappy or if one has certain desires or wishes that is reflected in their thoughts – these emotions as well may cause distractions. Distracting thoughts during prayers can be a wide variety, mainly due to what has been occupying the mind before.

Saint John, in the Paradise of the Fathers, was found by his disciple one day circling around the exterior of his cell several times, so he was asked what is happening. He

---

[30] Monastic living area

replied "a while ago I was in a discussion and I am trying to drive away the thoughts before they go into my cell with me." Therefore it is not only not only the solitude, but also what we expose our senses to. There is one who can get occupied with there own personal problems or other people's problems, either directly or indirectly responsible, but occupies themselves with it. Why waste your time and thoughts on that – is there nothing better to engage your time with? Saint Isaac, the Spiritual Elder said, "the person who talks too much is indicative of his emptiness within and thus fills up with such like idleness."

"WHERE AND WHEN TO PRAY"

HIPPOLYTUS OF ROME

Let every faithful man and every faithful woman, when they rise from sleep at dawn, before they undertake any work, wash their hands and pray to God. Then they may go to work. But if there is some instruction in the Word, they shall go there, considering that it is God Whom they hear in the one instructing. For having prayed in the Church they will be able to avoid all the evils of the day. The pious should consider it a great wrong if they do not go to the place in which they give instruction, especially if they know how to read.

If there is a teacher there, let no one be late in arriving at the Church where they give instruction. Then it shall be given to whoever speaks to utter things which are useful to each one, and you will hear things you did not know, and you will benefit from the things which the Holy Spirit will give to you through the one who instructs. In this way, your faith will be strengthened by what you will have heard. He will also tell you there what you ought to do at home. Therefore, let each one be certain to go to the Church, to the place where the Holy Spirit flourishes.

If there is a day when there is no instruction, let each one at home take a holy book and read enough of it to gain an advantage from it.

If you are at home, pray at the third hour and praise God. If you are elsewhere at that time, pray in your heart to God. For in this hour Christ was seen nailed to the wood (of the Cross). And thus, in the Old Testament the Law instructed that the showbread be offered at the third hour as a symbol of the Body and Blood of Christ. And the sacrifice of the dumb lamb was a type of the perfect Lamb. For Christ is the Shepherd, and He is also the bread which descended from heaven.

Pray also at the sixth hour. Because when Christ was attached to the wood of the Cross, the daylight ceased and became darkness. Thus you should pray a powerful prayer at this hour, imitating the cry of Him Who prayed and all creation was made dark for the unbelieving Jews.

Pray also at the ninth hour a great prayer with great praise, imitating the souls of the righteous who do not lie, who glorify God, Who remembered His saints and sent his Word to them to enlighten them. For in that hour Christ was pierced in His side, pouring out water and blood, and the rest of the time of the day, He gave light until evening. This way He made the dawn of another day at the beginning of His sleep, fulfilling the type of His Resurrection.

Pray also before your body rests on your bed (Compline).

Around midnight, rise and wash your hands with water and pray. If you are married, pray together. But if your spouse is not yet baptized, go into another room to pray, and then return to bed. Do not hesitate to pray, for one who has been joined in marital relations is not impure. Those who have bathed have no need to wash again, for they are pure.

By catching your breath in your hand and signing yourself with the moisture of your breath, your body is purified, even to the feet. For the gift of the Spirit and the outpouring of the baptism, proceeding from the heart of the believer as though from a fountain, purifies the one who has believed. Thus it is necessary to pray at this hour. For those elders who handed down the tradition to us taught us that in this hour, every creature hushes for a brief moment to praise the Lord. Stars and trees and waters stand still for an instant. All the host of angels serving Him, together with the souls of the righteous, praise God. This is why it is important that all those who believe make certain to pray at that hour. Testifying to this, the Lord says thus, "And at midnight, a cry was heard: 'Behold the bridegroom is coming!'" (Matthew 25:6).

Likewise, at the hour of the cock-crow, rise and pray. Because at this hour, with the cock-crow, the children of Israel refused Christ, who we know through faith, hoping daily in the hope of eternal light in the resurrection of the dead. With these things, all you faithful, if you do and remember them, instructing one another, and encouraging the catechumens, you will not be able to be tempted or to perish, having Christ always in your thoughts.[31]

"WORK IN PRAYER"

SAYINGS OF THE DESERT FATHERS

One of the brothers once asked Abba Agathons, "Among all good works, which is the virtue which requires the greatest effort?" He answered, "Forgive me, but I think there is no labor greater than that of prayer to God."

"MAKE ME WORTHY, O LORD"

SAINT ISAAC THE SYRIAN[32]

Make me worthy, O Lord, to behold Your mercy in my soul before I depart from this world. May I be aware in myself at that hour of Your comfort, along with those have gone forth form this world in good hope. Open my heart, O my God, by Your grace and purify me from any association with sin. Tread out in my heart the path of repentance, my God and my Lord, my hope and my boast, my strong refuge, by Whom my eyes may be illuminated, and I may have understanding of Your truth, O Lord.

Make me worthy, O Lord, to taste the joy of the gift of repentance, by which the soul is separated from cooperating with sin and the will of flesh and blood. Make me worthy, O Lord, to taste this state, wherein lies the gift of pure prayer. O my Savior, may I attain to this wondrous transition at which the soul abandons this visible world,

---

[31] *Apostolic Tradition*, 41.
[32] *Daily Readings with St. Isaac of Syria*, 37.

and at which new stirrings arise on our entering into the spiritual world and the experience of new perceptions.

"YEARNING TO PRAY"

SAINT CYPRIAN OF CARTHAGE

Dear brothers, the commands of the Gospel are nothing else than God's lessons, the foundations on which to build up hope, the supports for strengthening faith, the food that nourishes the heart. They are the rudder for keeping us on the right course, the protection that keeps our salvation secure. As they instruct the receptive minds of believers on earth, they lead safely to the kingdom of heaven.

God willed that many things should be said by the prophets, His servants, and listened to by His people. How much greater are the things spoken by the Son. These are now witnessed to us by the very Word of God Who spoke through the prophets. The Word of God does not now command us to prepare the way for His coming: He comes in person and opens up the way for us and directs us toward it. Before, we wandered in the darkness of death, aimlessly and blindly. Now we are enlightened by the light of grace, and are to keep to the highway of life, with the Lord to precede and direct us.

The Lord has given us many counsels and commandments to help us toward salvation. He has even given us a pattern of prayer, instructing us on how we are to pray. He has given us life, and with His accustomed generosity, He has also taught us how to pray. He has made it easy for us to be heard as we pray to the Father in the words taught us by the Son.

He had already foretold that the hour was coming when true worshipers would worship the Father in spirit and in truth (John 4:24). He fulfilled what He had promised before, so that we who have received the spirit and the truth through the holiness He has given us may worship in truth and in spirit through the prayer He has taught.

What prayer could be more a prayer in the spirit than the one given us by Christ, by whom the Holy Spirit was sent upon us? What prayer could be more a prayer in the truth than the one spoken by the lips of the Son, Who is truth Himself? It follows that to pray in any other way than the Son has taught us is not only the result of ignorance, but of sin. He Himself has commanded it, and has said: "You reject the command of God, that you make keep your tradition" (Mark 7:9).

So, my brothers, let us pray as God our Master has taught us: to ask the Father in words His Son has given us, to let Him hear the prayer of Christ ringing in His ears is to make our prayer one of friendship, a family prayer. Let the Father recognize the words of His Son. Let the Son Who lives in our hearts be also on our lips. We have Him as an advocate for sinners before the Father; when we ask forgiveness for our sins, let us use the words given by our Advocate. He tells us, "Whatever you ask the Father in My name, He will give you" (John 16:23). What more effective prayer could we then make in the name of Christ than in the words of His own prayer?[33]

---

[33] *De dominica orsatione*, 1-3.

"ZEAL IN PRAYER"

MAR EPHREM THE SYRIAN

When you see life's pleasures, beware that they might not distract you, for they conceal death's snares. Likewise, a fisherman casts not his hook to no purpose. As bait for his hook, the enemy uses the delusion of sensuality to arouse desire, that He might thereby catch men's souls and subject them to himself. A soul which has been caught to serve the enemy's will then serves as a snare for other souls, for it conceals the grief of sin with its apparent delight. While exercising the virtues, be not dejected by the labors involved, for there can be no virtue without labor. While laboring, lift up the eye of your soul and, as you contemplate that joy which is on high, you will not shrink from any task.

Praise to the All-Good One, Who because of His love has revealed glory to the sons of men! From dust did He create a voiceless being and adorn him with a soul, a proprietress of heavenly treasures.

He gave these lips of dust the capacity to magnify Him, so that through them all creation might sing praise unto Him. Come, you who are endowed with speech, let us sing praise unto Him until we repose in the sleep of death. Every night shall we contemplate death which will stop our lips and lay silence upon us. The righteous who spent their nights in vigilance live even after death; but the lawless, who reject the glory of the Son of God, are already dead while they yet live.

Let us rouse our bodies with psalms and spiritual hymns that we might join the wise virgins whom our Lord praised, and in vigilance behold His glory in the night that will cause the world to tremble.

Let us not wallow in pleasures, that we might behold His glory in the day of His coming. Let us stand before Him as watchful servants, ready for the hour when He will bring the sons of men to the judgment. The body that burdened itself with prayer shall soar through the air on the day of the resurrection; without shame shall it behold its Lord; with Him shall it enter into the habitation of light, where it will be cherished by the angels and by those who here burdened themselves with vigilance and prayer.

Blessed is He Who made us instruments of His glory and put exaltation in our unworthy lips! Praise be to His compassion, for He has made those who were of dust concelebrants with the angels, that every night and at all times they might praise His holy Name.[34]

---

[34] *The Spiritual Psalter.*

Ⲇⲟⲝⲁⲥⲓ ⲟ̀Ⲑⲉⲟⲥ ⲏ̀ⲙⲱⲛ

Printed in Great Britain
by Amazon

32249394R00036